Copyright © 2024 by Jacob Bruce Friest

All rights reserved.

No part of this publication may be reproduced, distributed, or transmitted in any form or by any means, including photocopying, recording, or other electronic or mechanical methods, without the prior written permission of the author and illustrator.
To request permission, contact Jacob Friest: friestjacob@gmail.com.

Book Cover by Victoria Shearham
Illustrations by Victoria Shearham

ISBN: 978-1-0690101-2-4

First edition, 2024

Toronto, Ontario
Canada

Nabi Origin: Nabi is short for Nabia, which is borrowed from the Nabateans. They were an ancient Arabic nomadic tribe who first settled in Petra, Jordan in the sixth century BC. Nabi was born in Amman, Jordan in 2019 and arrived to Canada in the winter of 2021. Her name symbolizes her home and pays homage to her birthplace.

This is a story about facing adversity and being resilient during difficult times. It is a lesson on finding the positive elements in life. *Nabi's Way Home* is about a brave young dog who had to endure many hardships and overcome many obstacles.

My wife and I rescued Nabi in 2021, but in so many ways she rescued us. Whenever I need extra strength and courage I think of Nabi's story, and will continue to even when she's gone. I use her tale to guide me through life's challenges and struggles, to carry on when things get tough, just as she did.

Her story is one of hope. A story that has provided me with a different perspective to see problems and the world at large. Nabi has gifted us with a way in which we can see all the good and positive things that life provides, even when things aren't going well.

Thank you Nabi, I am forever grateful you have entered our lives and touched our hearts.

Love,

Jacob and Andrea

Nabi's Way Home

Written by
Jacob Friest

Illustrated by
Victoria Shearham

This heartfelt story begins from a land oceans away,
where a sweet lonely puppy, began her life as a stray.

Where the city meets the sand,
she was born with her litter.

One day her family left,
she was scared and all alone.

There was no food or water,
not even a single bone.

Abandoned after her birth,
the streets were a scary place.

All she wanted was a home,
a happy and loving space.

One day she was discovered,
at an empty workers' site.
A man found a furry ball,
which then stirred to his delight.

He picked her up in his arms and brought her to a safe place. It was there that they noticed many wounds on her sweet face.

The shy frail girl needed aid
and months of medical care.
This part of her life is sad,
and extremely hard to bear.

Surgery after the next,
the vet worked her eye and jaw.
After several months surpassed,
a new beginning she saw.

Winky was the name given, for she only had one eye.
Winky was a miracle, for she kept on getting by.

Day after day without fail,
her carers saw her kind heart.
She made lots of doggy friends,
life was good except one part.

Winky needed a real home;
people to give her a shot.
During the height of covid,
a young couple claimed the spot.

They heard of her brave story
and knew Winky was the one.
The couple raised some money,
and the paperwork was done.

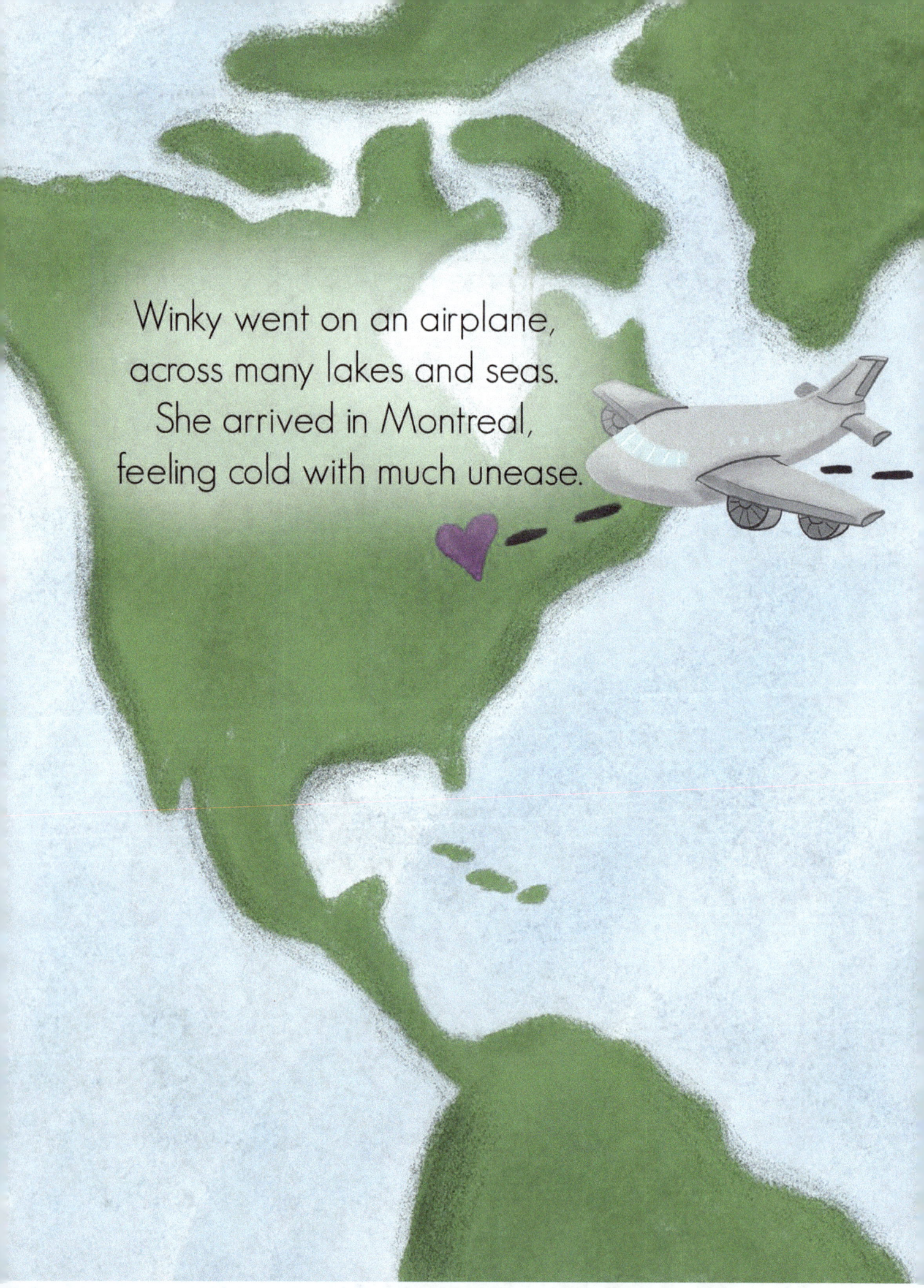

After the exhausting trip,
she pounced in the cold white snow.
Playing with her new humans,
she then frolicked to and fro.

They watched her play with smiles,
both the husband and the wife.
Winky grew strong and healthy,
she loved her new found life.

She enjoyed the fun ravines,
the beach, and all the seasons.

She chased after the squirrels and chewed sticks for no reason.

Winky then became Nabi,
which signalled a brand new start.
Nabia is for Jordan,
to keep home close to her heart.

She brought much joy to many,
as her story grew and grew.
Her life influenced others,
and of course her humans too.

Everyday with Nabi,
was full of laughter and glee.
Her cuddles made things better,
for the family of three.

Their lives became happier,
as their pain faded away.
Nabi had survived trauma,
yet she welcomed each new day.

She happily wagged her tail
and gave huge kisses and hugs.
She also liked to nestle,
on floors, couches, beds, and rugs.

As the year came and went by,
Nabi never gave a frown.
She was goofy and playful,
always a fun-loving clown.

Nabi helped others adopt, with her fame going around.

This meant more happy puppies,
after their new homes were found.

Nabi's tremendous journey
changed the way her owners think.

She has filled their deep dark void,
as she was their missing link.

Either Winky or Nabi,
her brave story will be told.

As her life continues on,
she'll be loved until she's old.

Being silly -2021

Beach fun -2022

Fun in the snow -2023

Snuggles with dad -2020

Nabi gets adopted -2020

Nabi's rescue -2019

East Coast Road Trip -2022

Halloween -2023

Best friend Roo -2022

Hiking with mom and dad -2024

First vet visit -2019

About Nabi

Favourite Treats- anything to do with fish, chicken, cheese and peanut butter (Yummy!!).

Least Favourite Treats- anything that is too dry, and basically any vegetable (I am a meat and cheese type of gal).

Favourite Place to Visit- the beach or ravine (I love running wild and free!).

Least Favourite Place to Visit- over crowded and overly noisy places, like big dog parks (they make me nervous!).

Favourite Thing to Do- get belly rubs and pets (dad says I am a big suck!).

Least Favourite Thing to Do- take a bath (followed closely by getting my nails trimmed!).

Best Friend- my neighbour Roo (she's a Mini Australian Shepherd).

Favourite Toy- any toy that isn't mine and that has been pre used (chewed and drooled on for extra flavour of course, or dad's stinky socks!).

Least Favourite Toy- brand new expensive toys that mom and dad buy (hehe!).

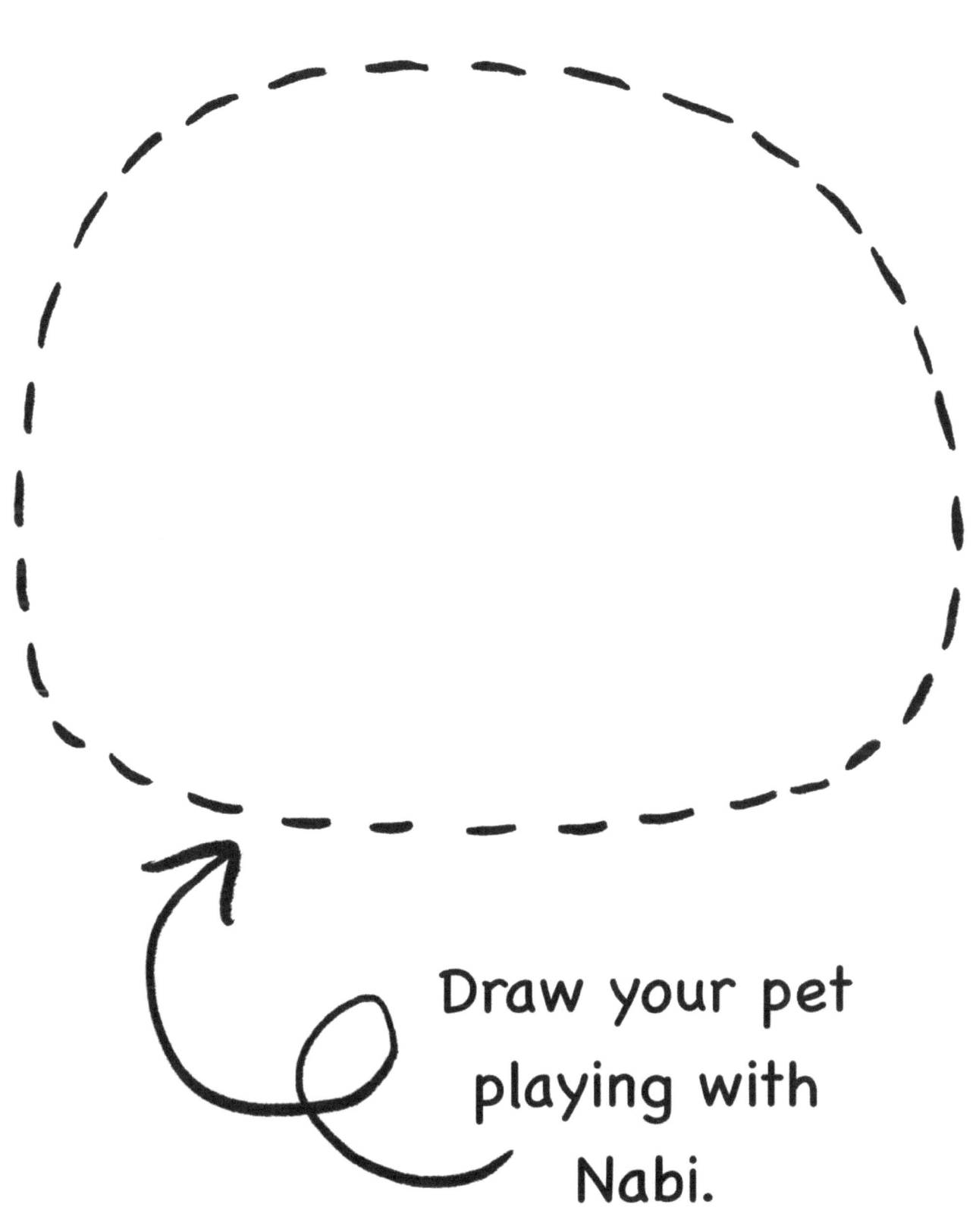

Draw your pet playing with Nabi.

Author

Jacob Friest was born in Windsor, ON and has been teaching in special education for over a decade. An avid reader and writer since he was young, this is Jacob's first children's book. He currently lives in Toronto, Ontario, with his partner and rescue dog, Nabi.

Illustrator

Victoria Shearham is an illustrator, author, and elementary school teacher. She has drawn pictures and created stories all her life. Currently, she lives in Toronto, Ontario, with her dog Ava.

www.ingramcontent.com/pod-product-compliance
Lightning Source LLC
Chambersburg PA
CBHW082023050526
44107CB00101B/644